Make Your Own Game Apps

-

For Kids

Volume I

second edition

Author: Krishna Balwalli

Illustrator: Ria Balwalli

ISBN-13: 978-1484994122

ISBN-10: 1484994124

Thanks for your encouragement :
John Lucyk , Wilson Elementary School
Melinda White and Jatin Shah, Seminole State College

For Ritika and Archana

3

Table of Contents

Introduction..1(

    From the Author...1

    For Parents and Teachers..1

    Can my kid do this?...1

    For Kids...1

    Web Site for this book 1

My First Game App...1

    What's a Game App, Huh?...1

    How will the App work, Show?..1

    Let's Start Already, Go!..1

    What are the Steps, Count!...2

    What are the tips, Tiptoeing?..2

Get the Tools..2

    Computer Needed, Computer!...2

    Need Internet Access, Please!...2

    Download from the Internet, Zoom!..2

    What are the Tools, Tools!..2

    Download the Tool Set, Set!..2

    Download the Recorder, Buzz!..2

    Give me some Tips, Tiptoe!...2

Setup the Tools..30

    Setup the Coder, Coder!..31

    Setup the Kit , Situp!...32

    Setup the Emulator, Emu!...33

    Setup the Recorder, Standup!...................................34

    Setup the Painter, Painter!..35

    Setup the Device, Optional!......................................36

    Give me some Tips, Tiptoe!.......................................37

Super Hero Drawing..38

    Draw a Super Hero, Yay!..39

    Scan the Picture, Help!...40

    Give me some Tips, Tiptoe!.......................................41

Super Hero Painting...42

    Painting the Picture, Color!.......................................43

    Resize the Picture, Size?..44

    Happy and Sad, Twins?..45

    Happy Super Hero, Happily!.....................................46

    Sad Super Hero, Sadly!..47

    Give me some Tips, Tiptoe!.......................................48

Super Hero Talking..49

    Laugh and Cry, Twins again?....................................50

Laughing Super Hero, HaHaHa!...51

Crying Super Hero, BooHoo!...52

Naming the names, Name!...53

Give me some Tips, Tiptoe!..54

Learn Coding...55

What is Coding, Cooking?..56

Time for some Code, Codeword?...57

About Code, Compile?...58

About Code, Run!...59

About Code, Method?...60

About Code, Storage?...61

About Code, Command?...62

About Code, Project?..63

About Code, Loading?..64

About Code, All Together!...65

Setup the Project...66

Make a New Project, New!...67

Making a New Project, New New!..68

Move Things Around, Move!..69

Setup the Code..70

Hey Code, Hey!..71

Hey More Code, Hey!...71

Hey Storage, Hey!...73

Hey More Storage, Hey!...74

Hey Method, Hey!..75

Hey More Method, Hey!...76

Hey New Method, Hey!..77

Hey More New Method, Hey!...78

Compile Code, Ready!..79

Give me some Tips, Tiptoe!..80

Load and Run the Code..83

Load and Run Game App, Run!..84

Between Happy and Sad, Click!..85

Give me some Tips, Tiptoe!..86

The Real Device..87

What is the Device, Cold Ice?..88

Export the Game App, Port?..89

More Export the Game App, Port?..90

Still More Export the Game App, Port?.................................91

Download to Device, Down!..92

Playing on the Device..93

Get Installer for Apps, Install?...94

Run on Device, Run!...95

More Run on Device, Run!..96

Between Happy and Sad, Tap!..97

My First App is Ready, Yippee!..98

Give me some Tips, Tiptoe!..99

My Second Game App..100

Better than First App, Yes!..101

More Super Hero Paintings..102

New Faces, Fun! 103

Funny Super Hero, Funny!...104

Angry Super Hero, Grrr!..105

Keep Quiet Super Hero, Shh!..106

Silent Super Hero, Silence!..107

More Super Hero Talking..108

New Voices, Fun Fun! 109

Laughing Super Hero, HoHoHo!...110

Shouting Super Hero, Shout!..111

Ssh Super Hero, Shh!...111

No Sound Super Hero, Nothing!..111

Setup the New Project..114

Reuse the Project, Reuse!...11

Move Things Around, Move Again!.....................................11

Setup the New Code...11

Hey New Code, Hey!..118

Hey Change Storage, Hey!..119

Hey More Change Storage, Hey!...120

Hey Change Method, Hey!...121

Hey Change New Method, Hey!..122

Hey More Change New Method, Hey!......................................123

Compile Code Again, Ready Again!...124

Load and Run the New Code..125

Load and Run New Game App, Run!..126

Between Six Faces, Click!...127

The Real Device Again...128

Export the Game App Again, Port!..129

More Export the Game App Again, Port!.................................130

Repeat Steps, Repeat!...131

Between Six Faces, Tap Tap!..132

My Second App is Ready, Fantastic!.......................................133

Ready for More Game Apps..134

More Super Heroes and More Voices, Go!..............................135

Enjoy your Apps, Happy!..136

What Next, Stay Tuned!..137

Introduction

From the Author

I thought of writing this book after my fourth grader Ria became interested in writing game apps. I guess her inspiration came from making up her own characters and then making a game out of it. I hope other kids can use this book and benefit from it to learn and enjoy making game apps.

For Parents and Teachers

If you are a parent or teacher reading this book then you can make it a reference book to teach your kids. Parents can setup some time at home and gather a small group and get them interested in making their own game characters. Teachers can use this book in their programming or gifted classes where the kids are already looking for fun challenging tasks.

Can my kid do this?

I wrote this book with keeping my fourth grader in mind so it is meant for kids around that age familiar with using a computer and interested in writing Game Apps. So as a parent or teacher, you can step in to help when needed and make it an enjoyable experience for your aspiring Game App makers.

For Kids

If you have always been interested in making

your own Game Apps then this is the book for

you. This book has all the steps for getting you

started so you can just relax and focus on the

characters that will go in to your Game App. Find

friends who are also interested as it is more fun

to discuss characters with each other. That will

help to make your character even more fun!

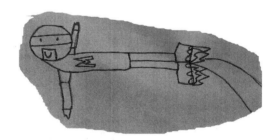

Web Site for this book

Thee is a book web site where you can find

lots of helpful information. The web site is

http://makeyourowngameappsforkids.com

You will also find code samples and information

about upcoming volumes of the **"Make Your**

Own Game Apps – For Kids" book series

which will have even more fun stuff to make

Game Apps.

My First Game App

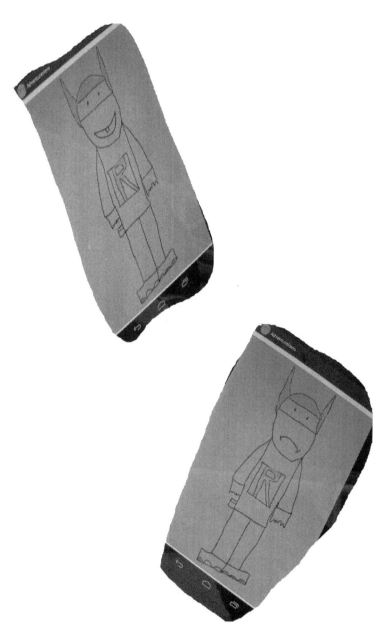

What's a Game App, Huh?

A Game App is a computer program. Think of it like a story that you would write with super heroes and adventures and other fun stuff. So you could write a short story or a really long story. But remember to always make it a fun story so you can enjoy it again and again.

How will the App work, Show?

The Game App will work just like how you would write a story. First you will imagine how your Super Hero character would look like and then draw it. Then you will put the character in to your computer and add some voice sounds. Then you will be able to see it work just like a real Game App.

Let's Start Already, Go!

First let us look at what we need to start our Game App. We can start with thinking of a Super Hero who has magical powers. Imagine how that Super Hero would look like. Imagine all the fun stuff that Super Hero would do and the adventures that the Super Hero could be in. Now that should set you thinking of all the fun that you can have with your Game App.

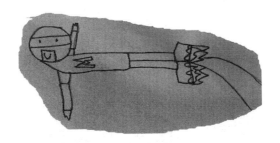

What are the Steps, Count!

The steps are pretty simple to follow. We will first need to gather some tools. Then we make up our Super Hero characters. Next we put the characters into the Game App. I have tried to make it seem really simple and it really is. All of the steps are described in detail in this book so you can just follow.

What are the tips, Tiptoeing?

Check the tips pages for help if you get stuck when making your Game App. So if you see a picture like at the bottom of this page then it means there are tips to help you. So look out for the tips pictures and go to the tips page if you get stuck. You can also get help at the book web site.

Get the Tools

Computer Needed, Computer!

A computer is needed. It could be a laptop or desktop and should have Microsoft Windows on it. We will use this computer to get some software and then make our Game App. Here is a Tip. Remind your parent or teacher that the "computer needs 2 GB or more of memory and 10 GB or more of free disk space" so that it is fast enough.

Need Internet Access, Please!

Before starting we need to make sure that

there is an internet connection to download

some software. So you can get help from your

parent or teacher to make sure that the internet

is up and running. It may take some time to

download the software so you may want to grab

a book to read while the download is going on.

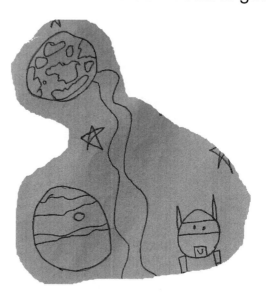

Download from the Internet, Zoom!

We are going to download software from some web sites. I have included the links for the downloads. If in case the link does not work then you can search that website as links on a website can change. After you download the software, you will be setting it up and then it will ready for use.

What are the Tools, Tools!

We will first need a **Painter** to paint our Super

Hero. Next we will need a **Coder** to put some

code for our Super Hero to do fun stuff. We will

need a **Recorder** to record voices for our Super

Hero. We will also need an **Emulator** to test our

Game App. We will also need a **Kit** to setup the

software.

Tips on Page 29

Download the Tool Set, Set!

We will be using **Android Developer Tools**

which has a **Coder** called **Eclipse**, the

Emulator called **Android Virtual Device**

Manager and the **Kit** called **Android SDK**

Manager. Here is the link that I used at the time

of the writing of this book.

http://developer.android.com/sdk/index.html

If the link does not work then search the website

http://developer.android.com

Download the Recorder, Buzz!

We will be using **Audacity** as our **Recorder**.

We will use **Ogg Vorbis** as our **Recorder**

Sound Format. Here is the link that I used at

the time of the writing of this book.

http://audacity.sourceforge.net/

If the link does not work then search the website

http://audacity.sourceforge.net/

Give me some Tips, Tiptoe!

Here are some tips to help you out.

Remember to check this and other tips pages

often if you feel like you are stuck. You can also

get help at the book web site.

- **Page 27**

   has the name of the **Coder, Kit** and the

   Emulator.

- **Page 28**

   has the name of the **Recorder** and

   Recorder Sound Format.

Setup the Tools

Setup the Coder, Coder!

To setup the **Coder**, go to the same folder

where you saved the Tool Set earlier. You will

see an **eclipse** folder and inside it double-click

on the **eclipse** application. Select a **Work**

Space by typing <u>C:\MYAPP</u> in the window. You

can make the workspace somewhere else too.

Next you will setup the **Kit**.

Setup the Kit , Situp!

Now you will click on the icon for the **Kit**. If you see an **Install Packages** button then click it and follow the prompts. You can now close the **Kit** by clicking on the top right X. Next you will setup the **Emulator**.

Tips on Page 37

Setup the Emulator, Emu!

Now you will click on the icon for the

Emulator. Then click **New**.

We will only change four things in the window.

For the first item from the top type in **MYAPP**.

For the second item select **Nexus 7**.

For the third item select the first option.

Type in 256 next to where you see **RAM**

Then select **OK** at the bottom.

Close both **Emulator** and **Coder** by clicking on

the top right X.

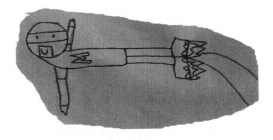

Setup the Recorder, Standup!

To setup the **Recorder**, Just double-click on the downloaded file and follow the setup prompts. You can then click on the icon to launch it. If you can see the window then the **Recorder** is ready for our use.

Setup the Painter, Painter!

To setup the **Painter**, First click on **All Programs** at the bottom of your screen.

Click **Accessories**.

Click **Paint**.

This will bring up our **Painter** window where you will be painting your Super Hero.

We will be using **PNG** as our **Painter Picture Format**.

Setup the Device, Optional!

T he **Device** is a tablet or smart phone that you would want to run your Game App on. This is the final step after you are done with making your Game App. The Device is optional so it is okay if you don't have it. My choice of **Device** for this book is **Nexus 7**.

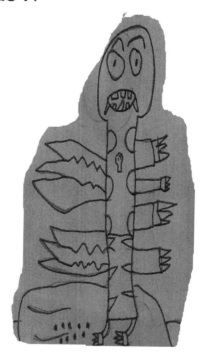

Give me some Tips, Tiptoe!

Here are some tips to help you out.
Remember to check this and other tips pages
often if you feel like you are stuck. You can also
get help at the book web site.

- **Page 32**

    When you open the **Coder**, if you don't see

    the **Kit** then click on **Window** to see it.

- **Page 35**

    has the name of the **Painter Picture**

    Format

Super Hero Drawing

Draw a Super Hero, Yay!

Take a sheet of paper and draw your Super

Hero. This can be any blank paper sheet. Make

sure that you use clear lines. Do not shade. The

Super Hero below is how your drawing should

look like. Leave the

mouth blank.

Scan the Picture, Help!

Now you will need to put your Super Hero into the computer. You can scan it with a scanner or you can take a picture with your digital camera and then put it in. Ask your parent or teacher for help with doing this. Once you see how it is done then it is very easy to add more of your drawings later on.

Tips on Page 41

Give me some Tips, Tiptoe!

Here are some tips to help you out.

Remember to check this and other tips pages

often if you feel like you are stuck. You can also

get help at the book web site.

- **Page 39**

    Use a black pen to trace over your **Super**

    Hero drawing so it looks nicer when you

    are scanning it.

- **Page 40**

    I used a digital camera and a card reader

    to put the picture in the computer.

Super Hero Painting

Painting the Picture, Color!

Open the picture that you saved earlier with

the **Painter**. You can make an outline around

your Super Hero or color inside. Just color only

what you want for now. You can always come

back later and make changes.

Resize the Picture, Size?

We need to change the size of the picture to a smaller size. That will help to get the picture to work properly inside the computer.

Click on **Resize**

Select **Pixels**

Type 300 for **Horizontal**

Vertical becomes 400 by itself

Click **OK**

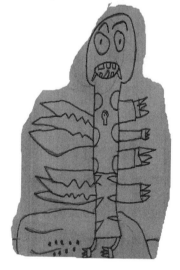

Happy and Sad, Twins?

We will now make two Super Heroes out of

one. They will be just like twins that is a Happy

Twin and a Sad Twin.

Go to **Computer** then **C** drive.

Make a new folder called **MYAPP** there.

We will be putting all our Super Hero stuff in this

new folder.

Happy Super Hero, Happily!

Remember we left out the mouth for our

Super Hero. So now we will make a happy

mouth for our Super Hero.

Select the **MYAPP** folder.

Type in **happy_p** and select the **Painter**

Picture Format.

Select **Save As** in the **Painter** and save to

MYAPP folder.

Your Happy Super Hero

should look something like

this picture.

Sad Super Hero, Sadly!

Now we will make a sad mouth for our Super
Hero.

Select the **MYAPP** folder.

Type in **sad_p** and select the **Painter Picture**

Format.

Select **Save As** in the **Painter** and save to

MYAPP folder.

Your Sad Super Hero

should look something like

this picture.

Give me some Tips, Tiptoe!

Here are some tips to help you out.

Remember to check this and other tips pages

often if you feel like you are stuck. You can also

get help at the book web site.

- **Page 44**

    If **Vertical** does not become

    400 then it is okay and leave as is.

- **Page 47**

    Press the **CTRL and Z** keys together to

    erase the happy face then start sad face.

- **Page 47**

    Remember to close the **Painter** when you

    are done.

Super Hero Talking

Laugh and Cry, Twins again?

So now we have two pictures for the Super Hero. To make our Game App exciting, we are going to put voices for the Super Hero. Since we have a Happy Super Hero, we need a laughing sound. For our Sad Super Hero, we need a crying sound. We will use the **Recorder** for this.

Laughing Super Hero, HaHaHa!

Start the **Recorder** and click on the Record

button to start the recording.

Laugh away for 5 seconds.

Click the **Stop** button.

Click on **File**.

Click **Export**.

Select the **MYAPP** folder.

Type in **happy_s** and select the **Recorder**

Sound Format.

Close the **Recorder**.

Crying Super Hero, BooHoo!

Start the **Recorder** and click on the Record

button to start the recording.

Make crying sounds for 5 seconds.

Click the **Stop** button.

Click on **File**.

Click **Export**.

Select the **MYAPP** folder.

Type in **sad_s** and select the **Recorder Sound**

Format.

Tips on Page 54

Close the **Recorder**.

Naming the names, Name!

Did you notice that we named the pictures and voices alike? We did that so it is easy to match the picture and the voice with each other when we put the code in. It will help us organize our code nicely with the matching pictures and voices.

Give me some Tips, Tiptoe!

Here are some tips to help you out. Remember to check this and other tips pages often if you feel like you are stuck. You can also get help at the book web site.

- **Pages 51 and 52**

  Make sure that the **"Internal Microphone"** shows on the **Recorder** if you cannot see your voice being recorded.

- **Pages 51 and 52**

  Click OK for any prompts. Close the **Recorder** without saving changes.

Learn Coding

What is Coding, Cooking?

Really Coding is just like Cooking. You first decide what dish to make. Then you pick your ingredients. Then you follow cooking directions. Then you cook the dish and it is ready to eat. So our dish is a Game App and we are going to use ingredients like Compile, Run, Method, Storage, Command, Project and Loading.

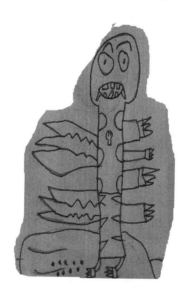

Time for some Code, Codeword?

If you want to know why we should do coding then the answer is to make the computer obey what you want it to do. If you did not put any code in then the the computer would not know what to do. So for a Game App, we will first put in some code and then tell the computer to follow the directions in the code.

About Code, Compile?

The computer does not understand English or Spanish like we do. So we have to give it code in a language it can understand. So **Compile** means to take English and change it to computer language. Computer language is not easy to read and looks like numbers and other characters put together.

About Code, Run!

How to tell the Computer that it should start

obeying the directions that you put in the code?

You do that by telling it to **Run**. So when you run

the code then the computer is obeying the

directions in the code that you put in.

About Code, Method?

Suppose you gave someone a piece of paper that had written on it "Walk straight two steps and then make a left turn". If you wanted to put something like that in code then you would put that in a **Method**. So a **Method** can have many things for the computer to do just like our piece of paper with directions.

About Code, Storage?

If you told someone to clean your room then you also need to tell them where to put things. So you could say that all of your shoes go in the shoes closet. That is the same for **Storage.** When you put code in the computer you need to tell where to put things. This helps the computer keep things organized and clean.

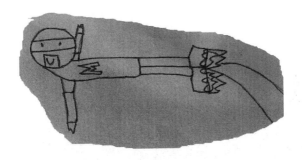

About Code, Command?

If you told someone to do something that they have to do then that would be a **Command**. So the code that you put in the computer will have commands for the computer to do something. We will be using **Commands** in our code for the computer to show pictures and play sounds.

About Code, Project?

If you went to the supermarket to get groceries then you use a shopping cart or a shopping basket to hold your groceries. A **Project** is just like that for code and holds all of your code together in a nice organized way so then it easy to work with.

About Code, Loading?

If you were at a party and about to eat some snacks the you would use a plate. You would load the snacks on the plate and then eat them. That is the same for code. When you **Load** the code, the computer then is ready to run it. So that is right before the computer can start obeying the directions in the code.

About Code, All Together!

So we looked at the ingredients that are needed in code. So for the Game App, we first get the **Project** ready. Then we put **Method**, **Storage** and **Command** in the **Project**. Then we **Compile**, **Load** and **Run**. All of the ingredients come together nicely in this way to make the Game App.

Setup the Project

Make a New Project, New!

Now we will make a new project. Start up the

Coder.

Click **File**

Click **New**

Click **Android Application Project**

Type **MYAPP**

Click **Next**

Click **Next**

Making a New Project, New New!

Now you can choose an icon for your Game

App.

Click **Circle**

Click **Browse**

Select the **MYAPP** folder from before

Select **happy_p** picture file

Click **Next**

Click **Next**

Click **Finish**

Move Things Around, Move!

Now we are going to move our Super Hero

stuff into the Project.

Go to the **MYAPP** folder

Click **happy_p** then press **CTRL** key and click

on **happy_s**, **sad_p** and **sad_s**

Type **CTRL** and **C** keys together

Go to the **Work Space** folder

Go to **MYAPP** folder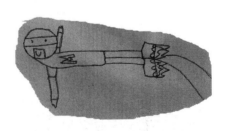

Go to the **res** folder

Make a new folder called **raw**

Double-Click on the **raw** folder

Press **CTRL** and **V** keys together

Setup the Code

Hey Code, Hey!

Now we are going to add some code to the

Coder.

Click on the **Coder** and press **F5**

Click on **src** under **MYAPP**

Click on **com.example.app**

Click on **MainActivity.java**

Hey More Code, Hey!

Next click on the tab for **activity_main.xml** so

now you can see the **MYAPP** screen

Click on the "**Hello world!**" that is under the

MYAPP screen

Press **Delete** key

Click **Images & Media**

Click **ImageView**

Drag it to the middle of **MYAPP** screen

Click **OK**

Tips on Page 80

Click next to **On Click** and type **taptap**

Press **CTRL** and **S** keys together

Hey Storage, Hey!

Now we are going to add storage for our

pictures and voices in the **Coder**.

Locate the first **{** at the top

Click right after it

Press the **Enter** key two times

Type the lines of code below

int idx = 0;

int [] pics = { R.raw.happy_p , R.raw.sad_p } ;

Hey More Storage, Hey!

There are a few more lines of code that we

need to type in.

int [ ] snds = { R.raw.happy_s , R.raw.sad_s }

android.media.MediaPlayer mp;

android.widget.ImageView iv;

Press **CTRL** and **S** keys together

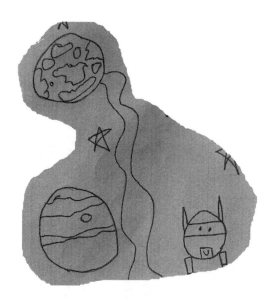

Hey Method, Hey!

Now we are going to put in some code for a

Method.

Click right next to where you see **main);**

Press the **Enter** key two times

Type this **Command** on the same line

iv = (android.widget.ImageView)

findViewById (R.id.imageView1) ;

Type this **Command** on the same line

iv.setImageBitmap

(android.graphics.BitmapFactory.

decodeResource(getResources() ,

pics [idx])) ;

Hey More Method, Hey!

There are a few more lines of code that we need to type in.

Type this **Command** on the same line

mp = android.media.MediaPlayer.create (getApplicationContext() , snds [idx]) ;

Type this **Command** on the same line

*mp.setLooping (**true**) ; mp.start() ;*

Press **CTRL** and **S** keys together

Hey New Method, Hey!

Now we will put in a new method called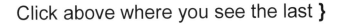

taptap.

Click above where you see the last **}**

Press the **Enter** key two times

Type this **Method** on the same line

public void taptap (android.view.View v) {

Type this **Command** on the same line

if (idx == 0) idx = 1 ; *else* idx = 0 ;

Type this **Command** on the same line

mp.stop() ; mp.release() ;

Hey More New Method, Hey!

There are a few more lines of code we need to type in.

Tips on Page 80

Type this **Command** on the same line

iv.setImageBitmap

(android.graphics.BitmapFactory.

decodeResource (getResources() ,

pics [idx]));

Type this command on the same line

mp = android.media.MediaPlayer.create

(getApplicationContext() , snds [idx]) ;

Type this **Command** on the same line

*mp.setLooping (**true**) ; mp.start(); }*

Press **CTRL** and **S** keys together

Compile Code, Ready!

T he Coder has already compiled the code. It

did that when you pressed **CTRL** and **S** keys

together. So now the code is already compiled

and ready to go. We will run the code next and

see the Game App in action.

Give me some Tips, Tiptoe!

Here are some tips to help you out.
Remember to check this and other tips pages
often if you feel like you are stuck. You can also
get help at the book web site.

- **Page 71**

  Check if **Coder** is already open.

- **Page 72**

  To see the **MYAPP** screen, click on the
  Restore icon on the left, which looks like
  two squares on top of each other.

- **Page 72**

  Click the maximize button of the window to
  make it easier to see the code.

- **Page 72**

  To see **On Click** use the scroll bar on the right to go down

- **Page 73**

  Click on the **MainActivity.java** tab first. Press the **Enter** key after you type each line.

- **Page 73**

  Press the **Enter** key after typing the code on the same line.

- **Page 77**

  Use scroll bar to locate the last **}** at the bottom.

- **Page 78**

  Click the **activity_main.xml** tab and press

  CTRL and **S** keys together

- **Page 78**

  Click the **MainActivity.java** tab and press

  CTRL and **S** keys together

- **Page 78**

  There should not be any red marks. A red

  mark means you have made a mistake

  when typing in the code so check it again.

Load and Run the Code

Load and Run Game App, Run!

Now we are ready to load and run our Game

App in the **Emulator**.

Right-click on **MYAPP** in the Coder

Click on **Run As**

Click on **Android Application**

The **Emulator** will open and start

The **Emulator** will load and run the Game App

Between Happy and Sad, Click!

You can move between the Happy and Sad

Super Hero pictures by clicking on the

Emulator. You will see that the Happy voice

plays with the Happy picture. Also the Sad voice

plays with the Sad picture.

Give me some Tips, Tiptoe!

Here are some tips to help you out.

Remember to check this and other tips pages

often if you feel like you are stuck. You can also

get help at the book web site.

- **Page 84**

  The **Emulator** will take a little time to start

  so just hold on. If the **Emulator** does not

  show your Super Hero then click on the

  lock and then unlock icons on the

  Emulator.

The Real Device

What is the Device, Cold Ice?

If you have a tablet or smart phone with you then you can download your code to it and run the Game App. You will have the most fun with your Game App by running it on the actual Device. I used the **Nexus 7** as my Device. If you don't have a Device, skip to Page 97.

Export the Game App, Port?

First we will take the Game App out of the

Coder so then it can be copied over to the

Device. So **Export** means taking the Game

App out of the **Coder**.

Right-click on **MYAPP**

Click on **Export**

Click **Android**

Click **Export Android Application**

Click **Next**

Click **Create new keystore**

Click **Browse**

Go to **MYAPP** folder

More Export the Game App, Port?

T here are a few more steps to complete the export.

Type **MYAPP.ks**

Click **Save**

Type **MYAPP123 for Password and Confirm**

Click **Next**

Type **MYAPP**

Type **MYAPP123 for Password and Confirm**

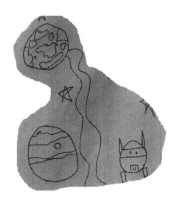

Still More Export the Game App, Port?

This is the last set of steps and we will be

done.

Type **25**

Type **MY APP**

Click **Next**

Click **Browse**

Go to **MYAPP** folder

Type **MYAPP.apk** and then **Save**

Click **Finish**

The **MYAPP.apk** file has our Game App and we

can download it to the **Device!**

Download to Device, Down!

Start up the Device and connect it's **USB**

cable to the computer. If you have not used **USE**

before then get help from your parent or teacher

Go to **MYAPP** folder

Right-click **MYAPP.apk** and select **Copy**

Go to **Computer**

Click **Nexus 7**

Click **Internal Storage**

Right-click and select **Paste**

Now disconnect the **USB** cable

Playing on the Device

Get Installer for Apps, Install?

These steps are done on the Device so you don't need the computer anymore for these steps. We have to download an **Installer** for Apps from the **Google Play Store**. There are lots of installers available and free ones too. Download the **Installer** and you are ready to do next steps. Ask your parent or teacher for help here.

Run on Device, Run!

We will now install the Game App using the

Installer.

Tap **Settings**

Tap **Security**

Tap **Unknown sources**

Tap **Home**

Run the **Installer** and select **MYAPP.apk**

Click **Install**

Click **Done**

Tap **Home**

Tap **Settings**

More Run on Device, Run!

There are a few more steps and you can then play your Game App.

Tap **Security**

Tap **Unknown Sources**

Tap **Home**

Tap **APPS**

Tap **MYAPP** icon

Your Game App will

now start!

Between Happy and Sad, Tap!

You can move between the Happy and Sad

Super Hero pictures by tapping on the screen.

You will see that the Happy voice plays with the

Happy picture. Also the Sad voice plays with the

Sad picture.

My First App is Ready, Yippee!

Congratulations! You just made your very first Game App. Now you know what is needed to make a Game App. I hope you enjoyed all the fun work with Painter, Recorder and Coder to complete and see your Game App actually working!

Give me some Tips, Tiptoe!

Here are some tips to help you out.

Remember to check this and other tips pages

often if you feel like you are stuck. You can also

get help at the book web site.

- **Page 95**

   For **Settings** Click the middle icon with the

   six dots.

My Second Game App

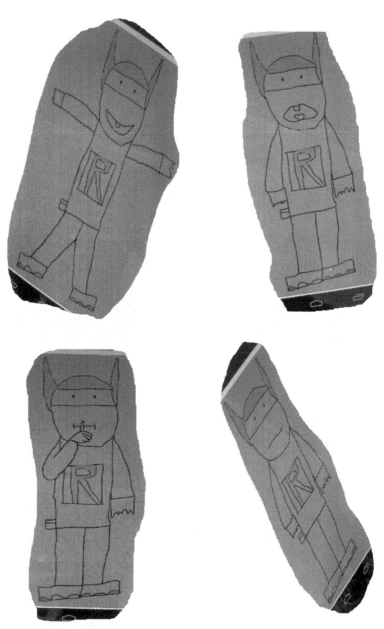

Better than First App, Yes!

It was real fun building your First App. But you can do so much more with your Game App to make it even more fun. So let us start working on our Second Game App. We will build more faces and voices so that our Second Game App looks and feels much much better than our First Game App.

More Super Hero Paintings

New Faces, Fun!

To make new faces, we will again use **Painter.**

The new faces that we will use are Funny, Angry,

Quiet and Silent. We already have Happy and

Sad. So that will give us a total of six faces for

our Super Hero.

Funny Super Hero, Funny!

Now we will make a funny mouth for our

Super Hero.

Select the **MYAPP** folder.

Type in **funny_p** and select the **Painter Picture**

Format.

The Super Hero below is how your Funny Super

Hero should look like.

Angry Super Hero, Grrr!

Now we will make an angry mouth for our

Super Hero.

Select the **MYAPP** folder.

Type in **angry_p** and select the **Painter Picture**

Format.

The Super Hero below is how your Angry Super

Hero should look like.

Keep Quiet Super Hero, Shh!

Now we will make a quiet mouth for our Super

Hero.

Select the **MYAPP** folder.

Type in **quiet_p** and select the **Painter Picture**

Format.

The Super Hero below is how your Quiet Super

Hero should look like.

Silent Super Hero, Silence!

Now we will make a silent mouth for our Super

Hero.

Select the **MYAPP** folder.

Type in **silent_p** and select the **Painter Picture**

Format.

The Super Hero below is how your Silent Super

Hero should look like.

More Super Hero Talking

New Voices, Fun Fun!

So now we have four more pictures for the Super Hero. Again to make our Game App exciting, we are going to put voices for the Super Hero. Since we have a Funny Super Hero, we need a funny laughing sound. For our Angry Super Hero, we need a shouting sound. For our Keep Quiet Super Hero, we need a shush sound. For our Silent Super Hero, we will not have any sound. Like with the first app, we will use the **Recorder** for this.

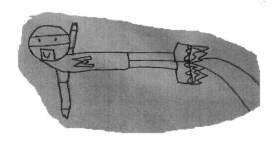

Laughing Super Hero, HoHoHo!

Start the **Recorder** and click on the **Record**

button to start the recording.

Laugh in a funny way for 5 seconds.

Click the **Stop** button.

Click on **File**.

Click **Export**.

Select the **MYAPP** folder.

Type in **funny_s** and select the **Recorder**

Sound Format.

Tips on Page 54

Close the **Recorder**.

Shouting Super Hero, Shout!

Start the **Recorder** and click on the **Record**

button to start the recording.

Make shouting sounds for 5 seconds.

Click the **Stop** button.

Click on **File**.

Click **Export**.

Select the **MYAPP** folder.

Type in **angry_s** and select the **Recorder**

Sound Format.

Tips on Page 54

Close the **Recorder**.

Ssh Super Hero, Shh!

Start the **Recorder** and click on the **Record** button to start the recording.

Make shush sounds for 5 seconds.

Click the **Stop** button.

Click on **File**.

Click **Export**.

Select the **MYAPP** folder.

Type in **quiet_s** and select the **Recorder Sound Format**.

Tips on Page 54

Close the **Recorder**.

No Sound Super Hero, Nothing!

Since our Super Hero is silent, there is no sound to record. We will remember to also make sure when we put the code in that there is no sound for the Silent Super Hero.

Setup the New Project

Reuse the Project, Reuse!

We are going to use the same **Project** that we setup in **Coder** for the First App. So that will save us some work. It is always a good idea to reuse code because that helps you to build on what you did before.

Move Things Around, Move Again!

Now we are going to move our Super Hero

stuff into the Project. Go to the **MYAPP** folder.

Click **happy_p** then press **CTRL** key and click

on **happy_s**, **sad_p**, **sad_s**, **funny_p**, **funny_s**

angry_p, **angry_s**, **quiet_p**, **quiet_s** and

silent_p

Type **CTRL** and **C** keys together

Go to the **Work Space** folder

Go to **MYAPP** folder

Go to the **res** folder

Go to the **raw** folder

Type **CTRL** and **V** keys together

Setup the New Code

Hey New Code, Hey!

Now we are going to add some code to the

Coder just like before.

Click on the **Coder** and press **F5**

Click on **src** under **MYAPP**

Click on **com.example.app**

Click on **MainActivity.java**

Hey Change Storage, Hey!

We are going to make some small changes to

the storage that we already have.

Change this line

int [ ] pics = { R.raw.happy_p , R.raw.sad_p } ;

to this. Type this on the same line.

int [ ] pics = { R.raw.happy_p , R.raw.funny_p ,

R.raw.sad_p , R.raw.angry_p , R.raw.quiet_p ,

R.raw.silent_p } ;

Hey More Change Storage, Hey!

There are a few more changes to the storage

that we need to type in.

Change this line

int [ ] snds = { R.raw.happy_s , R.raw.sad_s }

to this. Type this on the same line.

int [ ] snds = { R.raw.happy_s , R.raw.funny_s ,

R.raw.sad_s , R.raw.angry_s , R.raw.quiet_s

} ;

Press **CTRL** and **S** keys together

Hey Change Method, Hey!

We can reuse the code for the **Method** that

we put in earlier as is so there are no changes

for this **Method**.

Hey Change New Method, Hey!

We are going to make some small changes to

the **Method taptap** that was created before.

Change this line

if (idx == 0) idx = 1 ; *else* idx = 0 ;

to

idx++ ; if (idx == pics.length) idx = 0 ;

Change this line

mp.stop() ; mp.release() ;

to

if (idx != 0) { mp.stop() ; mp.release() ; }

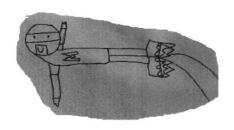

Hey More Change New Method, Hey!

T here is one more small change that we need

to make to the **Method taptap**.

Click right next to where you see

pics [idx])) ;

Press **Enter**

Type this line

if (idx == snds.length) **return** *;*

Press **CTRL** and **S** keys together

Compile Code Again, Ready Again!

The **Coder** has already compiled the code just like before. It did that when you pressed **CTRL** and **S** keys together. So now the code is already compiled and ready to go. We will run the code next and see the Game App in action.

Load and Run the New Code

125

Load and Run New Game App, Run!

Now we are ready to load and run our Game

App in the **Emulator** like before.

Right-click on **MYAPP** in the **Coder**

Click on **Run As**

Click on **Android Application**

The **Emulator** will open and start

The **Emulator** will load and run the Game App

Between Six Faces, Click!

You can move between the six faces Happy, Funny, Sad, Angry, Quiet and Silent Super Hero pictures by clicking on the **Emulator.** You will see that the proper voice plays with the proper picture. Only the Silent Super Hero does not have any voice.

The Real Device Again

Export the Game App Again, Port!

If you don't have the **Device** then skip to Page

133. We will again take the Game App out of

the **Coder** so then it can be copied over to the

Device. So **Export** means taking the Game

App out of the **Coder**.

Right-click on **MYAPP**

Click on **Export**

Click **Android**

Click **Export Android Application**

Click **Next**

Type **APP123** for **Password**

Click **Next**

More Export the Game App Again, Port!

T here are a few more steps to complete the

export.

Type **APP123** for **Password**

Click **Next**

Click **Finish**

So there were a lot less steps this time for the

export.

Repeat Steps, Repeat!

All you need to do is do the same steps as before.

Download to Device on Page 92

Run on Device on Pages 95 and 96

Now your Game App will have started!

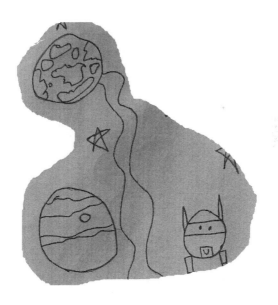

Between Six Faces, Tap Tap!

Yͭou can move between the six faces Happy, Funny, Sad, Angry, Quiet and Silent Super Hero pictures by tapping on the screen. You will see that the proper voice plays with the proper picture. Only the Silent Super Hero does not have any voice.

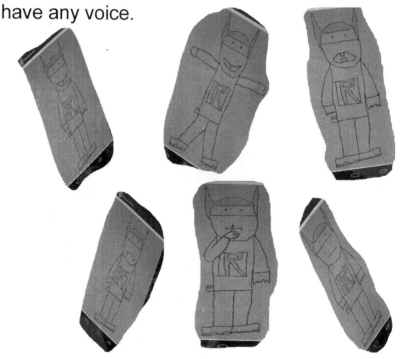

My Second App is Ready, Fantastic!

Congratulations again! You just made your Second Game App. Now you know what is needed to make a Game App having lot more features. I hope you enjoyed all the fun work with Painter, Recorder and Coder to complete and see your Game App actually working!

Ready for More Game Apps

More Super Heroes and More Voices, Go!

Our second Game App had a total of six

Super Hero pictures and voices. You can make

another Game App by adding even more

pictures and voices. You could even add sounds

and music instead of voices. Let your

imagination lead the way!

Enjoy your Apps, Happy!

When making a Game App, always be sure
to make it fun and enjoyable. That is very
important because if you cannot enjoy your
Game App then others would not enjoy it either.
Making funny Super Hero characters or funny
sounds or voices are easy ways to make a great
Game App.

What Next, Stay Tuned!

I hope you enjoyed this book as much as I enjoyed writing it. The possibilities for Game Apps are limitless so let your imagination guide you. Game Apps can become more fun by using backgrounds and Super Hero action. I am planning to include these fun features in my next book "**Make Your Own Game Apps – For Kids**" **Volume II**.

Good Luck for your Game Apps!!

25372581R00078

Made in the USA
Middletown, DE
28 October 2015